MARTIAN
THE SAINT OF LONELINESS

"Daring, open, and honest! Cagney's poetry beams beyond the surface but from the inner regions of his soul. From this depth, he radiates thoughts, feelings, and perceptions that are not only his but universal truths that we have in common. Do yourself a favor, buy, read, and experience *Martian: The Saint of Loneliness*."

Thomas Robert Simpson
AFROSOLO THEATRE COMPANY

"*Black Steel Magnolias in the Hour of Chaos Theory* was a masterpiece, and so is this book. These extraordinary new poems burst off the page, wild controlled explosions demanding our attention with their intelligence, frustration, wisdom, and love. James Cagney is one of our greats, an absolute gem of American poetry, thankfully hidden no longer."

Matthew Zapruder
AUTHOR OF *Why Poetry and Father's Day*

"I should probably say that in recent years some of my best poem listening moments have been afforded me by James Cagney, but don't get too comfortable. This poet uses language as corrective fluid, as antidote, as dream prompt and as spirit surgery. Yes, the pen is mightier than the sword because writers like Cagney will cause changes that you then have to live with. The poems in *Martian: The Saint of Loneliness* are sacred salt to be bathed in to cleanse, scattered in doorways and on windowsills for protection, and tasted in medicinal doses. The poems are also beautiful."

Kim Shuck
7TH POET LAUREATE OF SAN FRANCISCO

"James Cagney's voice is an arrow released with precision directed at the enemy. Employing irony, wit and truth-telling, Cagney explores his ancestral history in the USA and all the many injustices and lies he and his people had to endure and circumvent to survive. These are historical, social justice, and love poems of determination and sheer girth. These poems are a complete meal."

Opal Palmer Adisa, Ph.D.
DIRECTOR, INSTITUTE FOR GENDER
AND DEVELOPMENT STUDIES, UWI

"James Cagney writes with an explosiveness that is tempered by raw vulnerability. His words lay bare the gorge that separates myth and reality and force an unflinching look at inequity in the United States. His razor-sharp wordsmithing is painfully insightful and beautifully evocative. His poetry emits strength and fragility in equal doses as he explores love, loneliness, and loss. I will return to this collection again and again."

Elizabeth Gessel , Ph.D.
DIRECTOR OF PUBLIC PROGRAMS,
MUSEUM OF THE AFRICAN DIASPORA

"'History books have been set in the blood type of my family' James Cagney's book *Martian: The Saint of Loneliness* deftly synthesizes and articulates personal and ancestral rage against ubiquitous, systemic, and sadistic racism in these times and throughout time. The book is scorching and critical to exposing the gaping wounds of American racism, past and present. A mighty read."

Kimi Sugioka
POET LAUREATE OF ALAMEDA,
AUTHOR OF *The Language Of Birds*
AND *Wile and Wing*

"This work should be approached like a church doorway, reverently, humbly, and devoid of knowing.

Those who stop to pray here may never leave the sanctuary.

The service opens with an epic tale of self-construction of infinite dimension & dazzling scope, preparing one for baptism in Cagney's deep-water lyricism.

Cagney is revelation, swoon, and primal scream turned inside out.

From Queen Sophie making herself to the final sermon, you have the right to be remade.

Heartbreakingly beautiful,

hemorrhaging bitter blues-ed notes,

open for consumption,

at your risk,

for your pleasure."

Ayodele Nzinga

MFA, PH.D.,

POET LAUREATE, OAKLAND CA

ALAMEDA COUNTY WOMEN'S HALL OF FAME

YBCA 10, 2021-2022, MAPFUND, 2021

LBP, INC., BAMBD CDC

BAMBDFEST 2021 INTERNATIONAL

NOMADIC PRESS

OAKLAND

PHILADELPHIA

XALAPA

WWW.NOMADICPRESS.ORG

MISSON STATEMENT THROUGH PUBLICATIONS, EVENTS, AND ACTIVE COMMUNITY PARTICIPATION, NOMADIC PRESS COLLECTIVELY WEAVES TOGETHER PLATFORMS FOR INTENTIONALLY MARGINALIZED VOICES TO TAKE THEIR RIGHTFUL PLACE WITHIN THE WORLD OF THE WRITTEN AND SPOKEN WORD. THROUGH OUR LIMITED MEANS, WE ARE SIMPLY ATTEMPTING TO HELP RIGHT THE CENTURIES' OLD VIOLENCE AND SILENCING THAT SHOULD NEVER HAVE OCCURRED IN THE FIRST PLACE AND BUILD ALLIANCES AND COMMUNITY PARTNERSHIPS WITH OTHERS WHO SHARE A COLLECTIVE VISION FOR A FUTURE FAR BETTER THAN TODAY.

INVITATIONS NOMADIC PRESS WHOLEHEARTEDLY ACCEPTS INVITATIONS TO READ YOUR WORK DURING OUR OPEN READING PERIOD EVERY YEAR. TO LEARN MORE OR TO EXTEND AN INVITATION, PLEASE VISIT: WWW.NOMADICPRESS.ORG/INVITATIONS

DISTRIBUTION
ORDERS BY TEACHERS, LIBRARIES, TRADE BOOKSTORES, OR WHOLESALERS.

NOMADIC PRESS DISTRIBUTION
ORDERS@NOMADICPRESS.ORG
(510) 500-5162

NORTH ATLANTIC BOOKS' PUBLICATIONS ARE DISTRIBUTED TO THE US TRADE AND INTERNATIONALLY BY PENGUIN RANDOM HOUSE PUBLISHER SERVICES. FOR FURTHER INFORMATION, VISIT OUR WEBSITE AT WWW.NORTHATLANTICBOOKS.COM.

MASTHEAD
FOUNDING PUBLISHER
J. K. FOWLER

ASSOCIATE EDITOR
MICHAELA MULLIN

DESIGN
JEVOHN TYLER NEWSOME

Martian: The Saint of Loneliness

THIS BOOK WAS MADE POSSIBLE BY A LOVING COMMUNITY OF CHOSEN FAMILY AND FRIENDS, OLD AND NEW. FOR AUTHOR QUESTIONS OR TO BOOK A READING AT YOUR BOOKSTORE, UNIVERSITY/SCHOOL, OR ALTERNATIVE ESTABLISHMENT, PLEASE SEND AN EMAIL TO INFO@NOMADICPRESS.ORG.

COVER ART: "LIVING THROUGH STRANGE TIMES" (2004) BY WANGECHI MUTU, MIXED MEDIA INK, COLLAGE ON MYLAR 38 X 42 IN. AND 29 X 35 IN. DIPTYCH. © WANGECHI MUTU. COURTESY OF THE ARTIST AND GLADSTONE GALLERY

ARTIST PORTRAIT BY ARTHUR JOHNSTONE

Martian: The Saint of Loneliness BY JAMES CAGNEY IS PUBLISHED BY NOMADIC PRESS, A NONPROFIT, COMMUNITY-WOVEN PUBLISHING HOUSE HEADQUARTERED IN OAKLAND, CALIFORNIA. IT IS DISTRIBUTED BY NORTH ATLANTIC BOOKS, AN EDUCATIONAL NONPROFIT BASED IN THE UNCEDED OHLONE LAND HUICHIN (AKA BERKELEY, CA) THAT COLLABORATES WITH PARTNERS TO DEVELOP CROSS-CULTURAL PERSPECTIVES, NURTURE HOLISTIC VIEWS OF ART, SCIENCE, THE HUMANITIES, AND HEALING, AND SEED PERSONAL AND GLOBAL TRANSFORMATION BY PUBLISHING WORK ON THE RELATIONSHIP OF BODY, SPIRIT, AND NATURE.

FIRST PRINTING, 2022

LIBRARY OF CONGRESS CATALOGING-IN-PUBLICATION DATA

TITLE: **Martian: The Saint of Loneliness**
P. CM.
SUMMARY: AMERICAN HISTORY GOT YOU DOWN? ARE YOU FEELING ALIENATED? JOIN POET JAMES CAGNEY IN HIS BLISTERING SECOND COLLECTION, Martian: The Saint of Loneliness, AS HE JOURNEYS THROUGH TIME, SPACE, AND MEMORY WITH CAUSTIC, SATIRICAL BEAUTY. RECALL AMERICAN HISTORY THROUGH ITS SPENT SHELL CASINGS! TURN FAMILIAL GHOSTS INTO ART VALUABLE FOR GENERATIONS! IN THESE FULLY CHARGED POEMS, JAMES CAGNEY STORMS THROUGH AMERICAN FIELDS BLOOMING WITH ARTILLERY AND ANGER ON HIS THIRSTY QUEST FOR LOVE, PEACE, AND ACCEPTANCE, IN THE SMALLEST, MOST PRECIOUS GESTURES.

1. POETRY / AMERICAN / AFRICAN AMERICAN & BLACK. 2. POETRY / AMERICAN / GENERAL. 3. POETRY / SUBJECTS & THEMES / DEATH, GRIEF, LOSS. 4. POETRY / GENERAL ?

LIBRARY OF CONGRESS CONTROL NUMBER: 2022941660

ISBN: 978-1-62317-770-6

MARTIAN

The Saint of Loneliness

MARTIAN

The Saint of Loneliness

James Cagney

**NOMADIC
PRESS**

Oakland · Philadelphia · Xalapa

FOR YOU,   THE DEAD

contents

III.

IV.

reading guide
notes & acknowledgments

foreword

I've known James Cagney since 1994, and from the moment I met him I was always struck by his sweet disposition and compassion. He was always friendly and accommodating and one of the few American Africans I'd met since I arrived in California who was willing talk about the history and culture of people from other parts of the world.

We met at Laney College's audio/video lab. He was the overnight programming tech. I was a producer of a show called *Culture Shock News* that broadcasted on the college cable channel. My show interviewed a cross-section of artists, writers, musicians, and academics, mostly people of color from the Americas and around the world. Each told their culture-shock story of coming to and living in America. James helped me with the editing of my show, and on one infamous evening he screwed up an edit that had me furious. However, it was a measure of the man that he didn't panic and persevered in correcting the problem. It is often only when people are under duress that you learn of their inner qualities, their essence. James and I became fast friends.

Sometime later, I ran into him at the La Pena club in Berkeley. I was there recording slam poets for the San Francisco National Poetry Association video festival. I was the director of the annual video festival, and we invited video poets from around the world to submit their works and augmented the annual show with live recordings. I was surprised to see James step up to the microphone and perform. He'd always struck me as a very shy guy, and yet here he was blasting out a poem called "Ebonic Plague," with astonishing bravado. The poem was a reaction to the Oakland School board wanting to introduce Ebonics as an official language in schools. The controversy created a national hysteria, bringing black and white intellectuals from around the country to Oakland in defense of American English—whatever that is? James' performance was electric, and it set him on a path to local celebrityhood. We worked together on a video of the poem which was featured in several national film festivals, significantly, the Mill Valley Film Festival, which was an important venue for local and international artists at the time. This was years before YouTube, when producing and editing videos was a laborious process, needing dedication and creativity.

Our friendship was and still is based on mutual respect, though we don't always share the same beliefs. Our conversations were not debates but honest interactions of ideas that offered a platform to express ourselves and to be heard. What really cemented our friendship was our mutual admirations for two Bay Area legends, Piri Thomas and Reginald Lockett. Piri Thomas' book *Down These Mean Streets* made him a celebrity in 1967 as the first Latino to express his life's struggles in Spanish Harlem. Reginald Lockett's *The Party Crashers of Paradise* chronicled the American African world of West Oakland in the 1960s and 1970s, "accentuating," as Al Young commented, "the inner spirit of the black man in America." For James and me, these two icons inspired us to create and blossom in our own ways. They provided the validation and encouragement for us to believe in our creations, even before we knew what they were. They offered the true gift of the artist —faith in the possible.

I later discovered that James had honed his poetic vision and craft in Above Paradise, a club in San Francisco where artists were encouraged to experiment and explore. I wasn't a part of that scene, but I recognized the power it gave James as he continued to perform at La Pena and other venues in the Bay Area with astonishing verve and creativity. I collected his poetry broadsheets and sponsored him to be a part of San Francisco's National Poetry Association's "Celebration of the Word," headlined by Maya Angelou in 2000. James did this piece called "Spreading the Disease of Poetry," which even today I find astonishing and cathartic. I once chided him as the master of metaphor, wondering aloud if there was any meat in all those comparisons. I later realized that I was displaying my own prejudices, not his. And this situation illustrates James's compassion. He doesn't judge, belittle, or degrade anyone. He's like a mirror that reflects a deep soul, and shows with his poetry pathways of discovery—allowing the reader to find their own platform, take a rest, look around, and view our often-dysfunctional world from new and startling perspectives.

We are living now in dystopic times where the scent of our humanity is being extinguished daily by the burning fires of radical evil. Social, cultural, and political courage is required to stand up and grasp the burning honesty that is displayed and presented in James Cagney's poetry. To read James Cagney's poems is to reach for one's humanity, compassion, and love. Please join me.

Ian C. Dawkins Moore
AUTHOR OF *The Pandemic Blues*

introduction

Several years ago I attended an exhibit of work by Robert
Rauschenberg at SFMOMA. I hadn't heard of him before. At the
time, I worked in an office I despised that was two blocks away from
the museum, so I bought a membership and took leisurely, late
morning walks through the galleries.

His work ran the gamut of expression, from sculpture to
performance art. I spent the most time with his collages and
paintings, and it was while examining his work that I asked myself,
"How can I write like this?"

I've asked myself this question in several galleries while
standing before many different works of art, both famous and
undiscovered. Friends in poetry to whom I've confessed this argue
that I already paint with words. So what am I saying to myself? What
does that thought mean?

Standing before a painting or a perfectly timed photograph,
a feeling is transmitted. That feeling may be awe or confusion. But
more often than not, what gets transmitted to me is a feeling of
being thrilled. To my eye, it's the thrill of mixing media with ideas
and passion, rendering the world through a unique lens, and finding
something new within the familiar. No one is thrilled over clouds or
grass on a lawn. Those images only become thrilling when rendered
by hand in art.

Painters and poets have similar goals. Life becomes so routine
that people stop seeing and appreciating it. Artists want to engage
audiences and have them reconsider the familiar. People rarely
question the familiar. In bowing at the work of a painter and asking

myself, "How can I write in this way," I'm asking the universe for a kind of freedom. My personality likes order, method, and process. It takes work for me to let go and play, and it's a kind of work to release the poems into their own autonomy and logic. Maybe the real question is, "How does one let go with purpose and passion?"

Perhaps, this book is a gallery to explore. Some pieces might thrill you, others not so much. There is work here addressing police violence, guns, xenophobia, and death. These poems are childhood memories, erasures, dreams, meditations, and shouts into the void. Parental guidance is suggested.

James Cagney

HER MAJESTY QUEEN SOPHIE

(after artist Mary Sibande)

Her Majesty Queen Sophie
ordained beneath a halo of empyreal elements
Created herself   from herself

Every particle   hair   thread in phototropic dance
Her aura of elemental beads and bracelets
feathered   lured   baited with lavender

Right eye sun   Left eye moon   Third eye Horus

Attuned   Atoned   A crystal microphone

                        A golden triangle, sacred and immortal

Her rainforest of locks power lines transmitting spirit
Gospel mouth seeding black puddling earth
with fertile ululations
                    Her first praise song
A rain-bowing sail unfolding midair
colors from her throat ripening
into their own weight and logic.

Her Majesty Queen Sophie
did not bother with Adam or Eve
instead roasted a root ball
that opened, steaming, into family
the poured foundation to a pyramid of divinity.

Her Majesty Queen Sophie
had a premonition—
She saw a fatally wounded country

headless, hemorrhaging multitudes
chained for sale, cutting swaths thru
the desert

a collapsing landscape trembling with greed.

She saw the silky fabric of the ocean
fevered, jellied with blood
chanting unfinished prayers
in its foaming mouth.

She saw shaman toss a murmuration of sankofa birds
　　　　　towards a chalkboard sky
　　　　　　　　becoming notes on sheets of sacred vapor
　　　　　　　　　　　only god could read.

She saw a flotilla of vessels like wedding cakes
bloated with spectral bridegrooms
as death offered its ceremonial benediction
before jumping its own broom.

Her Majesty Queen Sophie screamed livid about the future.
She saw land more valued than the orphaned people on it.

She wept: *There's no appropriate trade for any dead*

Then watched ships stumble drunk thru the fog
towards a land of fevered infants screaming
in black bassinets behind a crib-wall of bones.

She stepped forward after them
as planets went retrograde, bowing like soldiers.

Crossing the threshold of the ocean,
She spread her apron beneath an armada of ships
shedding its dead weight of shadows
in ribbons of crimson bubbles.

Imagine a school of volcanic sparks
too hot to evaporate in the gelatinous
atmosphere of the Atlantic.

Come elements! Come assemble!
Let this day turn on divine behavior, she says
waving her apron seiner
beneath spirits shaking off their debt to life—
                        bodies falling in spent casings.

She flung them up into the blue black canopy of space
Elevated spirits crocheted into the digital graph of eternity.

A convoy of the disappeared assumed into a corona of stars.

This a version of corrective rapture
        rapture with purpose
              at history's altar

Ending in drones of kente cloth kofis as an asteroid field

Each a heart   a hearth   an ancestral campfire

left burning on the porch
to guide kinfolks home.

I.

U HAVE THE RIGHT

You have the right to be right. You have the right To Claim, To Rename, To Redefine. You have the right To Judge / To Frisk / To Choke. You have the right To Remain standing, To Remain whole, without being questioned. You have the right To Ignore others' rights. To Speak for all victims and tell a room of widowed mothers To Shut up.

You have the right to Not See Color and firebomb diversity out of your field of vision. You have the right To Invade, To Displace, To Demoralize. You have the right To Feel easily threatened. You have the right to the right side of history and To Enjoy the good weather of a touring oppressor.

You have the right To Trivialize the memorials of our dead while your missing daughters are canonized   their schools closed and festooned with roses.

You have the right To Be Inconvenienced by protests, by funerals, by the lives you didn't approve   You have the right To Ride to hounds To turn lynching into a fraternal hazing workout   To turn lynching into a pop-up shop or video game app and award souvenirs.

You have the right To Not See the problem   To browse safari thru our communities. To love wild animals while dismissing grown men as savages as monkeys.

You have the right To Prefer a comfortable lie over the truth.

You have the right To Claim genocide as culture, To fellate weapons and sponsor the indignity of war; to see war as a product, To Copyright its blood.

You have the right To Justify torture and take selfies with the dead. You have the right To Be both the victim and the knife in the dark; To Be the dark itself and the light glinting off the blade; To Be Ubiquitous and unseen.

You have the right To Ethnically Cleanse Until Culturally Clean and Repeat. You have a right to misunderstand history *just enough*, then edit the facts that make you uncomfortable.

You have the right To Condescend, To Humiliate, To Desecrate; To Redefine words used against you and dismiss our testimony; To Control our prescriptions while telling us we're crazy.

You have the right To Riot in the name of football; torch buses and dumpsters not in your backyard—whether you win or lose; anarchy is good fun! Boys being boys! and all ...

You have the right To Not Be Questioned; to never be held accountable. To in fact do the accounting! To Claim what hasn't been offered.

You have the right To Shoot and Not to Be Shot. You have the right To Demand God act on your order with the *Power of Now*. You have the right To Complain when our prayers get too loud.

If you ask me to swear on the Bible, I have the right to ask if you've read it.

Anything in your history can but will never be used against you.

Knowing and understanding that if you cannot remember which of your grandparents were members of the Klan, then your history will be expunged.

You have the right To Hope your enemies don't read history. You have the right To Have No Enemies. You have the right to close your door on their grievances.

You have the right not To Be Sorry. You have the right To Be Armed and assumed innocent. You have the right To Protect your best interests. You have the right of way. You have the right To Be Right.

FOUND IN AMERICA:
BAD APPLES

American history is the story of demonic possession.
Servile killers of sinister power.
Mass murderers divinely blessed and guided
to manifest their own destiny—
which involved enslaving and killing millions.

Satan wears the other's face.
Others have always been expendable
since they stand in the way of the American
Gods' imperial march to war—
wars sponsored and red carpeted
wars waged over fuel and false flag operations.

Most Americans write off unprecedented state terrorism
as a series of aberrations carried out
by bad apples.

                    Bad apples torching cities of civilians
                    to death with cluster bombs of napalm.

Americans charbroil cities under infrared ashes and uranium tar,
then go to lunch
possessed by the delusions of our own
God-blessed-goodness. We grew up
under the bomb, under orders (whose orders?),

then discriminate against radiated ethnic children
leaving them to smolder for decades and die
while we giggle-hide under desks
then wax nostalgic about Black Rain over mimosa brunch.

For Americans, innocence is a secular faith.
Brain rattling games our national religion.
What are we really?

Hyenas with polished masks,
conical incisors and fangs alternating
red, white, blue. Red as blood.
Blood on every street corner.

Blood tides on the shoreline
Blood in our pockets—Blood on the tracks.
Blood on a former mother's dress.
Blood on her face.

AMERICA, I AM

I come from the kidnapped,
                    the assaulted—
my country 'tis of reparations as in-store credit
                    backordered to bankruptcy

It is me & my trophy wife
passing as a dream of some kind

All I want is 40 dead mules
& an acre of land w/ a lighthouse
        right above the porch of the great Atlantic Ocean
            just in case any of my ancestors tasted nasty & made it.

I come from a people who pay a penalty every sunrise
& divinate to paroled gods with rancid hog maws.

The stripes plowed into my grandfather's back
will have to stand in for our family album.

Somebody threw some stars at my grand-momma's head
& said *'betcha won't ask for no freedom no mo'!*

Natives in prison-issue war bonnets say:
I come from a poisoned land that recycles children
        into artillery shells
                & where dark skin is good as

an invisibility cloak

until the police arrive.

I am proud to be a _____
where I can hold my head up and drown
in the downpour of state sanctioned cancer.

I am proud to hold my place
in back of the line.

I come from a land that's open all night
like a shotgun wound.

& as for ya'll tired,
                    ya'll poor
                              ya'll huddled masses
yearning to breathe free

Fuck ya'll!

I come from a place promising
a burning cross in every yard

& two meth labs in every garage
          & when I say: meth lab

I mean golden
          retrievers smoking crank.

The country I come from

I can flash all its gang signs
        & beatbox all their anthems.

I come from a place—
actually, I don't know where I come from

I just know I woke up here.

My babies were gone.
My house was on fire.
& I couldn't breathe.

IF YOU SEE SOMETHING, SAY SOMETHING

I pick up my mail down the street from an ICE raid,
hamboning myself for title, proof of ownership
passport, license. The sky began hailing handcuffs
& zip-ties, unlocked chains made easy for self-service.
I prayed like a sprinkler, my back drizzling every God with blood.

I open my mailbox downwind from an ICE house.
It resembles an overstuffed bird cage sweating feathers.
The house leaks, its windows spit long knots of people.
Children rap the Patteroller chant in Spanish while hopscotching.
My box weeps smeared postcards, prayers returned to sender.

I open my ICE box downhill from a cage of zombie birds—
it rattles with weeping mothers under siege by evil spirits
snatching ~~men~~ children out of families easy as pick-
pockets. They plead for my help but I'm dead already.

I open an extinct bird downtown from a male raid.
Its corpse whistles ancient work songs when squeezed,
while its chest spills continents of the undocumented.
I scream stop but ICE chips spew from my throat
only to quickly roll away, feeling threatened.

I open my mailbox downstairs from a chorus of ICE'd birds

in a prayer vigil around a ~~child~~ man lying in the street, near
extinction. It is as if he'd fallen from space and landed here,
leaking meteors. A speed-bump suicide. I turn him over & he asks:
What color am I? I don't have the heart to tell him.

BULLET GUMBO

"If bullets exploded into flowers
                    maybe my sons' effigy of ashes + clay
would be worth it."

                —Every new parent
                handed a birth and death certificate
                stapled together

In some communities, **this is** health insurance.

o

Look
        I'm going to ... puff up like a bird and chirp

For those easily triggered

        STICK 'EM UP, MOTHERFUCKERS

As you exit,
double-check that the body you're stepping over in the street
isn't someone you know.

o

    Ask Siri: How can I get home without being victim or
witness to gun violence?

After Processing, your device will leak a kombucha
of white tears

ALLOW | IGNORE | CANCEL

o

You know what's tired?

Memorial chalk outlines every Black History Month
stenciled outside gentrified coffee shops for English bulldogs only.

America scrubs its streets clean of history
I mean ...
America scrubs its streets clean with coppery bodies
                                    loofahs = afros
                                    Same difference

ASPHALT ANGELS!   **ASPHALT ANGELS!**

Limbs like arms on a crazy clock
that has no idea what time it is:

Right now? Or 200 years ago?

o

"I can no longer tell the difference between a casket and a crib,"
                                    Grandmomma says

She done started knitting chalk outlines
                she sees them more than flowers.

She say—"the lilies springing from the holes in his chest
smell like old churches full of out of print bibles."

o

        If evolution is real, then
we're one generation away
from a girl birthing a baby
with bullet holes already in it.

Not *birthmarks*, more like ricochets.

It'll be an ignored miracle.
You may have to watch the news all night.

o

ASPHALT ANGELS!!

Limbs extended into star points
        beneath a tableau of cops
                arranged like doubters
                        in every renaissance painting
                    of a doomed Christ

o

Every rookie knows Death is Certain
                                    & Heaven is Not

... that's what makes a bullet an easier citation to write

                              o

                              ASPHALT ANGELS!!!
Bullets full of holy water!
Passed out like placebos at the trap house

            To inoculate against crime—or—blackness
                                    which-ever's first.

                              o

It may look like Grandmomma is praying
but she's drafting obituaries like team stats.

A journalist once paid her in a shotgun shell
full of okra seeds and asked:

Q: How can you find so much sorrow in such a small space?

She started counting a mental rosary of graves and said:

A: "Here's what's so terrifying about tenderness
            Being the last one left to feel anything."

                              o

"Is it true guns don't kill people?"
                        Grandmomma asked her doctor.

Confusion kills people.
Fear kills people.
Hatred kills people.
The first people armed are usually confused, afraid and full of hate.

Her doctor said: Only if the gun is loaded with cancer! *Tee-hee*

Grandmomma knelt down to pray
        Then raised her hands where God could see them.

Artillery Father / Who Open Carry Off The Shooting Range / Hollow-
Point Be Thy Name

Her doctor said:
Take 2 bullets every ten minutes until it stops

o

If your God's not armed, you're going to the wrong church.

When the preacher shouts: *Is you been baptized?*

He means: Show me your bullet wounds—
the little puckered keloids
where Christ has kissed you!

o

Every Mass shooting—and by Mass
        I mean 'Form of Warship'—
is an infomercial for the NRA

followed by Pop-Up Gun Shows

bringing all the boys to the yard
faster than girl scout cookies.

○

The streets were filled the other day
with young people marching in protest

desperate to end gun violence.

If their teachers had been armed
there would have been no protesting ...

There, in fact, would be little difference
between going to school   or

being held hostage.

If a school loses a child to an armed teacher
the family will be awarded

     ○ 10 minutes on Good Morning America
     ○ A Certified Death Diploma
     ○ An Engraved Memorial Desk with
        the child's name and likeness airbrushed in graffiti*

*NOTE: THIS OFFER NOT AVAILABLE IN ALL SCHOOL DISTRICTS

o

... Is it true guns don't kill people?

Depends on if you consider gun-based suicide:
    1) Waste of a bullet—or—
    2) The Ultimate Act of Patriotism

o

If you had to show a gun
as form of I.D.
then the phrase would be:
"Unarmed Immigrants."

o

These are challenging times
with difficult questions to ponder

Why don't you ...

    o Come out to the balcony for some un-oppressed air

    o Step up to the podium

    o Step out of the car with your hands up

That's not rain, that's blood plasma.

The answer to all these riddles is dry firing from the sky.

BETWEEN A ROCK WALL AND AN IMMIGRANT

(after Allen Ginsberg)

America—goddamn.

This is what it's like being between Plymouth's
            Rock Wall and an immigrant

America, Liberty and Justice sure do make cute baby-goat names
America, your wig is powdered with coke but the lice don't seem to mind

America, I'm leaning in
I'm waiting for the conversation to turn to genocide so I can say
            ME TOO

America, wake up————————You're missing the point

You invented terrorism but only use dark skin models in its ad campaigns

You award assassins with Black Friday arms deals

America, when I say You, I mean *We*
            the People, I guess.

I planned to make extra cash trademarking
                    waterboarding
        but it's patented already.

Are there tortures you don't profit from?
To which bank do you entrust your Thoughts and Prayers?

America, can you say her name?
            As in a novena, not a marketing slogan.

America, 9 people were murdered in a church
but the shooter on your flatbed truck missed lunch

11 people were murdered in a synagogue
but they brought it on themselves praying unarmed

20 children were shot at Sandy Hook
but your taste is for a loaded gun
over a living child

If you say you love children,
Emmett Till has 4 little girls he'd like to ask you about.

                Here I go—bringing up old shit, again.

America, you pass blood hand to hand,
            generation to generation.

Has it ever occurred that YOU might be the savage,
            the terrorist,
the outside threat you're most afraid of?

Ask the Dakota Sioux their version of our history

Ask the buffalo about their endless pains

Ask the poisoned dead about the true
meaning of Thanksgiving

Don't act like you don't know what I'm talking about.

You dropped the compassion units
from all your mindfulness classes

America, what do we tell our children
about this home of dead braves?

What do we tell our children, period.

America, you had a great idea, once.

You're a dry drunk.
You throw a bomb then hide your hand.
You're the main suspect and loudest victim.

Stop, Children ... What's the sound of a Maglite
hitting a migrant's skull?
This is not setup for a bar joke.

This is me wondering why people are still crossing deserts
to escape slavery and oppression only to meet a walled promised land.

In 1987, President Ronald Reagan demanded

Soviet leader Mikhail Gorbachev: *Tear Down This Wall*
dividing East and West Berlin.

After all these years, it never occurred to me
that we kept those bricks in storage.

America, you're a big foster home where
the poor comes in for its abuse.

It's possible that the people who've passed the
Naturalization test know more of American history
than you do

        and they still want to live here.

America, kneeling was once viewed as a sign of respect
or surrender / a sign of honor / a pledge.

When a black man kneels, the gesture becomes *threatening*

America, *There I go, / There I go / There I go* ...

America, can you just   say her name?

Any name. Insert a name here:_____.
Like voting someone off your island

America, this year my therapist
recommended I get a facelift.
I misheard her say race-lift.

America, every time a siren rings
a black man gets his wings
and his mother kneels at an open casket
to sing the national anthem.

God's heart bursting—a napalm cherry—midair

What would it look like?
Who would we be if we had
no one left to hate, or ban?
Can you imagine this with your eyes open?

PHANTOM PAIN

For anything to be made
something must be broken open

I am a collage of every cracked vessel
I am a sheet of glass shattered back into sand

I am every mother   I am an artist

My breast once held and fed children
Now it nurses ancestral grief

      My experiences have pulverized me and yet my grains persist

My wound is a phantom limb with which
      I sketch and paint

I dip my brushes into homemade ochre tears while oceans
of elders instruct me with their spectral gospel

History books have been set
      in the blood type of my family—
          It is a text that never dries,
              its oldest pages smearing like
                 fresh mosquito bites

In most families, men are as easy to lose as keys or lighters

      Just ask my father

We lost him to a tall tree and a short rope
        It's why I cry whenever the wind chimes the leaves
of trees in parks   named after dead civil rights leaders

For example, this park once percolated with children
Now it's just the rubber dandruff from where something has been erased

I aim to fill the erasures   while art police
      critique my sons into the ground
          —killing in the other
    what they can't kill in themselves

In my work, I migrate
from Michigan to Missouri, collecting loose remains of
young men—an ear from Detroit, an eye from Chicago,
a hand from Pensacola; scattered through every street
like half smoked cigarettes

In front of this liquor store, for example,
40,000 eyes watched my son vanish into aerosol
and collectively said Nothing—
assuming him Untitled   Unvalued at auction

In every city blackness is an easy target
Too often there's more material than can ever be used
Too many memorials mushrooming in cities collapsed into
complacency

They used to say: Blacks don't feel any pain—
            so what's a little murder among neighbors?

I come from a people who stand accused of being black
            of wanting   to matter
We know if you stare at a canvas long enough
something breaks the surface
pushing the blankness until blackness appears
                              like a cereal of bullets

I am an artist. These streets are my studio—and here are my tools:

2 cups malt liquor blood
A plethora of preferred acids
1 cup hair (natural weave substitute, ok)
1 pkg Skittles (uneaten)
41 shots (of liquor, or tears, or whatever)
1 teaspoon of Newport or weed ashes

Combine into a batter until names of minor saints stutter your tongue.
Become angry and feel helpless. Call the police if you're feeling suicidal.
Question who is being protected and who is being served.
Bake in a studio apartment in a neighborhood of the disappeared
for an entire summer
            until the screaming toddler in the background forgets
            what she's crying for.
Season to taste with your open wounds. Mine are like rare flower petals,
            a kind of eczema unique to loss.

Don't let your white hand know what your black hand is doing.

Serve and keep serving fatherless children from a plate piled high with stars.

QUESTIONS FOR ART STUDY

1)   Where Does Art Come From? (In What Room Does Your Art Take Place?)

The painting decides for itself to happen
To assume every hue of blue and green layering the ocean—
            drawing pattern and feeling from the edges of space
down to the rusted truck fender mincing ministers into splotches of paint.

The canvas writes its own story
inventing a Rorschach spill of unpronounceable letters—
electrical language with different accents in each corner.
It assumes the shape of a leaping lion with a golden aura.
Its inkblot landmass of color spreading while you watch it—
                              blinking flirtation to its edges.

I turn myself into a living canvas so I may be re-written
I turn myself into a living canvas on which my mourning can be articulated

When you raise your face to the heavens, the stars resemble nuts and bolts
holding the sky together. I use whatever's around
to build something   that holds me together.

2)   How Do We Inhabit Ourselves Within A Gallery?

My charcoal sugar skin is not priced for retail.

My children will not break out in crime.
My family does not rhyme with bags of trash.
My hair does not belong in your hands.
My body is not your tool.
I am not temporary. I am not your nigga. I am not a hashtag.
I am not to be overlooked. I am not a victim.
I am not a nail anxious for your hammer.
I am. I am fragile, but will not shatter under your touch.

I Am.

Look at my raised chin—do you see the helm of an armed ship, or the
barrel of a loaded
        weapon?
Look at my pride, my third eye of laser light.
Among this stolen furniture in the house of the oppressor, I stand eternal
supported by my own skin. I stand like the word I was once
promised. I stand for those imprisoned by caskets. I will stand until my toes
dissolve away into nonsense
an impatiently scribbled signature.

3)   What Does It Mean?

This abstract painting is trying to recall something
trying to wake up.

It knows the textured kiss of rust.

Breakfast of nipples
Acrobatic black eyed peas dancing in a juke joint of hot broth
A thing wanting to be touched and touch back.

Surreal hallucinations in the bush   dinner of dark matter
            bending lightning into letters   designing tribal tattoos
                mountain ranges on the backs of elders
                        how you'd prep a plot of land for a garden.

Whatever isn't obvious is left to the subconscious & its weird random choices.

Go back and look at the summer '69—tell me what's the color of love.
That same summer, in our hood we hadn't finished mopping up
                                                the blood of kings.

Could murder be a form of art? Ask the police about the canvas of street
            unfinished corners invite conversation, not criticism.

 4)   How Much Is It Worth?

Hostage to history and its habit of expectations.
Look at what I've lost and tell me how much would you pay? Wait!
What about these children? Why are you burying our elders before they're
dead?

Ask yourself: Who is running the gift shop in our museum of blood?

Who will get the money Who will collect the taxes Who will laugh running
to who's bank How many receipts do we need to redeem the dead How many
empties before we've earned redemption Where's our leftover change from this
broken bill of rights
                How much is enough How much is too much

How much needs to be poured into your hands before you have the decency
to say stop?

II.

SATURNALIA

Zeus must be laughing his ass off
watching me chase Calliope's brassy calves,
their church bell praise song somersaulting in the air.

Lord, you done caught me ridin dirty.
High stepping my obedient emptiness
hustling to be filled with something fortified & warm.

Since my body-prison brewed its way thru puberty,
there remains a compound of failure in my blood.

Let me not remain so sensually challenged,
illiterate in every language 'cept the blues.

My tongue, losing its intimacy with words,
mistaking touch for rupture
or lust with lethargy,
or etc., or etc.

Never before have I rattled with so many impatient corpses.
Never before have I needed so little from a stranger.

To be recognized! To be handed a thing gently!
A dollar's change palmed back to you
as if it were an altricial hatchling!

For certain strangers, I am easy kindling,
my ashes sweet to taste.

Just ask the Saint of Loneliness about my labyrinth of weddings.
Ask my dead about the witchcraft of memory.
Ask my hands the origin of their humiliating nicknames.

They stay in my pockets
while I hike mile-long steel & glass canyons
passing several identical, uncrowded coffee shops
just to stand in line & briefly see you,

worship at the altar of your legendary eyes
—famous only in my private theater of cruelty—
& spin my rings around your fingers' soft ballet
over all my hardened denominations
that resist being broken down.

The smallest prayer I got on me is:
Our Father, What's wrong with me
& it remains un-cached beneath
this mirroring sky that never stops falling.

How you looked up, genuinely surprised
that any word strung between us was worth keeping,
even as its suggested promise was not.

A promise with the same weight
as the gossip & dirty limericks
eighth grade boys salt each other with
in their clubhouse patois.

I remain unnamed on your tongue
as any of the problematica & spittle
in the vinyl compilation spinning colors around Saturn.

Thus, my desire for anything reaches across to you

unanchored, unanswered, unwanted.

Yet, who besides me has ever offered to hold the sun through your
embrace?

Let me bite the brassy spark igniting the chasm between us
& plunge my nostrils into your lotus blossom afro
with the slam dance of a bee
in a ball-house of pollen.

The fibers of flaking stamens
sprinkled like crumbs of atoms
in your stargazing eyes.

Your lips, dewey from narrating
privately-screened dreams.

Dreams: small town playhouses that parody waking actions,
cabarets blinking from orange to indigo
to magenta & back in twilight darkness.

Its ecstatic soundtrack, a nervous bird in man's rib-cage,
my mouth harmonizing with rhythms
loud as a river's choir

psalming a sacrifice
to be drowned
in its desperate skin.

Your complicated dreamscape
ending in morning reflections
that approach & admire you first.

You, steaming, fragrant as fresh bread.

To find purchase in the world!
Any part of the world with you in it
raw, naked as a vegetable,
electric fibers erect & reaching

all sticky, sweaty with earth—
your bouquet conflated
in a promissory blossom & ooze.

To go any further, I will have to inquire your expectation of lips'
sugar.

What pushes the simplest song into a hymn?
What triggers desire to go viral
What vein sustains it?

What lures anything to burst forth blooming
[April's Black Currant? Sagebrush Buttercup?]
Can I drink from you to resize me
[Goldenrod? Cullumia? Crimson Columbine?]
What visions might your fermented nectar reveal
[Camasia lily? Bluebeard shrub?]

Along my face, light-waves
—like severed butterfly wings—
are a mockery of beauty.

I'm a demoted planet spinning,
melting in an un-mopped corner of space.

I'm a bygone reptile that hungers
prescription truffles & flora of the body.

I'm drawn & fluttering under your black light
of lichen hairs, lightly salted

cinnamon hot, bold & buttery
perfectly foamy & fresh

holding a spring's yield of aggressive rouge,
dimpled lacquer,
shouting nature by its myriad names.

With my hair snagged in your thorny fingers,
your tongue bookmarking my bible,
I break out in Pentecostal devotion.

Where have all the maps of bliss promised to lead:
the shower & scrub of ultra violet pollinators

the ecstasy
of scratching every itch
at once

my skin's unfinished spit shine
beneath the complex solar halo
of your caramel eyes

holdingmedown

captive, captivated
broken open & drowned
in teasing, tonguing petals.

Bucking across an operatic keyboard of sighs,
notes of varying touch.

What have you done to me?
What have you done through me?
What have you done with this amused stillness?
This thawed river?
This silent garden of eyelashes?
What solves the riddle of my true name?

I eat children down to their spongy rind,
tongue tender— sucking salted skin
clean as crayfish, loud and desperate,
my mouth dripping emptied bodies:
what remains after sucking gunpowder out of red, hot shells.

III.

LOVE IS EASIER THE HEADLESS WAY

after Rene Magritte's *Le Duo* [THE LOVERS] 1928

Love is easier the headless way
what good is desire in a world
where there is only a thriving darkness

Your mouth is a gate
opening to any place away from here—
the crumbling mansion of my nothing heart

With this form-fitting cloth
                              I do wed

Let us spill into one another
like waves of agitated milk
Placing our thoughts elsewhere
              onto unavailable others
while our useless arms
disappear into what frames us:

bench / bed / brothel of the mind

Everywhere we turn
winter remains unfinished

You don't trust your mouth
and I don't trust anyone
who says they love me

What are we willing to emotionally
barter for when all we have
is the simple meat of ourselves

And who can say what color the world
was before the earth's canvas
began flowering paint.

I have this recurring dream

where we live nameless as mushrooms
in the shadow of primeval birds—
birds who eluded ornithologists
and didn't want the press

But who agreed to soar forever
without landing
and seed the earth with minerals of light.
I awake, usually, in a choking grief.

How we've agreed to love one another
without ever opening our eyes.

ODE TO
A DESICCATED OLIVE

When the Greek farmer plopped
you plush and pregnant into my palm
he explained that when shucked
of your meat and pounded gently,
your pit excretes a mild antibiotic

Instead I carefully stirred you between
rudder and wave of my churning fingers, then
let you exhale on the countertop like a weeping battery

Beneath your crown of leaves
a pubescent froth curls and naps
with an acrid cologne of wood smoke

Left to simmer above time's distracted watch,
you dimple and age into an amber compass
pointing like a nipple to the tongue's north star

I caress the grand-mothered keloid
of your consecrated surface
so that you may come to Jesus
on my altar of breath

Remind this tongue how once
an engorged earlobe was combination
lock opening a soprano's scale of moans

Unfold your map of flavors
from vine to the secular intersection
of oil and bread

Medicinal and mythical,
you are a clairvoyant paragraph
punctuated with blossoms
of aspirin and eyelashes

If you take the place of my heart
let my veins be the roots of the tree
that brought you here

This   is like asking
the rain in your lover's hair
to fall back through the sky

INTERVIEW
WITH A ROSE

curved as a lip pouting for a kiss

sponge of sunlight,
my tiniest
filaments stand in ceremony
to your song of color

insects decide to walk the labyrinth
of your perfumed path

are you tickled by these
cellular inspectors
sipping your sweet wine of particulates

would you have preferred to be a robin
burdened with the sky's
most unique song

do you wish you were the moon
a whole planet of petals
with an atmosphere of cologne

a dolphin bathing in the coral medicines
of an oceanic garden?

you itch
when you are closed
   shy & anxious

unconcerned with weather
   death or dementia

you are the earth's soldier of love,
     desire

yet—what do you know of it?

ODE TO MY TOWEL

panel of fabric
　　　you hold
　　　a recipe
　　　that's escaped my parents

in your neatly tilled fields
a sugared soil
of soap foam & sebum
the chemical equivalent
of memory

　　　soft, blind bird
you know me
　　　better
than any lover

you
eat my tears
foul & fevered

　　　your amphibious wings
coast the beachhead of my body
made buoyant by
what flakes to ash everyday

harvesting grain
from my dream-swept
eyes, your form follows
the contours of my cheek
with a velvet bowl
of shaving foam

you know my nipples
      by name
the frayed wild weeds
bristling at my ears
the peppery base notes
of my darkest caverns

your indifferent body
is a loyal tongue
grooming the downy
underbrush of earth

dried or soaked
through you
i am born anew

have i ever thanked you
for your witness
your endless labors
      from sage to sugar

PERSONAL FOREST

I stood on the ledge
of the bathroom sink
      irritated, resolved

my mother's clippers
a growling chainsaw
in my hand.

I recalled my cousin—
seven years older—
who humbly bragged
over three fresh pubic cords
he found freshly minted
falling through his fingers.

      When I lowered the curtain
before the vaporous afro
my body produced in the dark

he exploded in Tex Avery debris—
all rubberized limbs, spring-loaded eyes.

Then later, over a mouthful of Apple Jacks,
diagnosed: *Glands!*
Maybe thyroid. Something like that.

Later that summer
when his older brother
caught glimpse of the black lichen
blurring the surface of my stomach,

he pounced like an arachnid
twirling   testing   pruning
with smiling white nails—
demanding *how*, and if
any leftovers
                    remained for him.

No boys
generated as much body hair
                              as I did.

                    Not even my father

who, every night one season,
watched my mother
cure my pre-school back & belly
with a marinade of calamine & zinc.

So—

in the name of friends
I would never make
                    and attention

I did not want in the new
junior high showers

I sheared myself.

Soft, curling fleece
snowballed
            tumbling
down my stomach
spiraling silently into the still
            pond of the toilet.

                    The clippers
left chalk-lines
down my chest & abdomen,
scratch marks correcting
a wrong answer.

This is the first time I
remember ever wanting
to hide
part of myself.

I wanted to be nondescript
like the others.
So Fresh. So Clean.

TOGUNA AT 61ˢᵀ AND MARKET

My father's blood followed the current of the street

spawned, too—apparently.

Any time daddy wasn't home, he'd be

Down The Street

had a secret life there

where they   breathed blue   90-proof air.

In those rooms,

his defrosted heart

circled his chest   like a catfish.

Down the street   was some 9 blocks south—

and a reservoir of filth, to my mother's taste.

Bottom feeding old drunks noodling nothing

in an open garage

an appointed RV

a diesel exhausted living room.

Drunks from my dad's longshoreman days.

Haggard and greying drunks

Falling bones and bullshit drunks

A grapevine of drunks

A bullpen of drunks

A stagger of drunks

Burdened with crossroad prophecy in blues harmonica

Waggling in like bees from fresh nectar juke joints.

From the hour school let out

till long after the sun   hung over its noisy, belligerent sea.

A kind of sea shimmered between the old men.

A black whisky sea

A sky latticed with Lightnin'

     Hopkins   A murder of Old Crow bourbon

     unscrewed and squawking.

HOUSE OF SLAMS
AND HOLLERS

who occupies the storefront houses at the crossroads
shotgun houses like abandoned churches

one house slouched behind the musty aroma of trees

windowsill radio chatters like a bird on caffeine
the living room smells swampy with ashes and bottle caps
kitchen of vintage graveyard-shift coffee   boiled viceroys
cicadas with exoskeletons of brandy
and chickens chained in the backyard

night turns over haunted with moths

air cooled with shuffled decks
and howling hounds missing hell

the methane of certain ghosts
gets drawn like window shades
dealt in   poured shots
at this place where the road crosses its legs
                        like a gentleman

here lies the uncharted territories of some blues
stigmata blues   razorblade blues

blues for lips just out of reach
blues screaming blouses of plaster down bedroom walls

choirs of apocalypse blues ignite the red wicks of their tongues
sing harmony to calm bluegill river
for Saturday's baptism of hot lead

dawn rises with fire on its mind, takes off its top hat

names drip from his mouth in comets, false crosses

anything not already on the ground
              holding on, praying
done grabbed a guitar, a shotgun   and ran

HOW TO OPERATE HEAVY MACHINERY

(circa 1978)

1. Think of yourself as a medical specialist puzzling over the diagnosis for a machine's stubborn silence, its symptoms of tremors and smoke.

2. Dip the doughnut of your torque converter into a steaming cup of black oil. Stainless steel carbide bologna sandwiches. Fan belt licorice. License plate soup.

3. A bowl of lug nuts bubbles the red milk of transmission fluid like tadpoles. Brackets and spark plugs breach greasy cookie jars on your automotive spice shelf.

4. Examine the patient through a stethoscopic sheet of Marlboro smoke, an x-ray on a light-board. Translate the fevered gibberish of an engine in idle.

5. Let the sun pause before your workshop to hang stars above the door. Ignore the son and his failing starter. Consider you might be a better god to a society of steel. Know how to put them in their place.

6. Give yourself a fuel treatment. Lunch of bourbon on kerosene rocks. Brake Fluid ice cream. Backfire of kick-started beer cans spewing.

7.   Witch doctor with a ratcheting wrench through your nose—your ignited blue hands assemble metallic dreams.

8.   There is no better mattress than cardboard on a sidewalk or driveway, Rorschach patterned in oil, a crunch of sand sprinkled as before a tap-dancer. Your wife and son know this, too...

Stranded on the porch, watching you, ready to run.

FINANCIAL DISTRICT CONFESSIONS

Showing up is what we do for work.
Especially on slow days of empty conference
rooms of souring coffee and St. Louis
bagels latticed into arguments.   At my old job
at least we had chess or Deuces. Afterwards,
my boss would call me into his office
for emergency meetings on Death
Rides a Horse, Cemeteries
Without Crosses, The Great
Silence.   One opens
with a gunslinger dragging a coffin
on a rope through the mud.
My boss would talk a long while
then cuss apologetic, I Gotta Take This.

        After our office moved,
for two weeks I had no desk.
I was a full-time consultant on race & trivia.
Oh, there were boxes & binders
& blood & sweat shorting
out my headphones & iPod.
                    But on many days,
I'd clock in, tell a joke, prescribe a movie
—then leave. I'd walk to bookstores since
 there were bookstores.

Once, instead of wheatgrass,
I bought a box of hot french fries
for the kids downstairs at Juicery
and every Friday thereafter
the shift manager would go to the freezer
and pour me a shot glass of whiskey.

Alcohol warps the drink cups, he said.

But mostly, I would return
to the shell of our former life & hang out.
    Two whole floors to myself.
I'd sit in their corner offices & cry or meditate.
I'd piss in the ficus & do a sun salutation
then walk back to work to tell my boss
everything I knew about John Ford.

WICKED GAME

Oklahoma flatlands. Night's rich perfume of lightning and oil. This, back when I was clairvoyant in music videos. I'm with my cousin who's driving on a knife blade of asphalt neatly slicing the tundra. He appears fixed, rigid. He hard-stares into the blue-black screen of sky tuned to nothing. We're together this week due to death and blood, both strands sagging loose between us. We are family without having ever been friends. Perhaps the true death is not his grandmother, but himself, since his heart remains this week in the purse of a woman who can no longer be bothered. This empty plated landscape, licked clean of any footprints, is the perfect metaphor for all I've ever known of love. But before I can figure anything out, just then, a sudden guitar calls order from the radio. Between the silences we pass back and forth, the car fills with strummed notes, a swirling phantom embroidering the air. *Sometimes*, I said, gently parting our curtain of silence, *when I hear this song, I imagine an astronaut, bouncing along moon rock like a yo-yo in slow motion, away from the crumpled spaceship he's just been tossed from. And in the distance, beyond the crash, planet earth turns perfect and silent as he crawls back to his smoldering vessel, his face a shattered web of blood.*

Some people, he said to the highway, just see things different.

TRIGGER WARNING

Having always preferred funerals in the rain

       the casket, a shell—the body, a seed
sprouting wild from any garden of ravens.

This one a cemetery in Oklahoma
—the land flat as a plate of petroleum.

A troop of clones file out of a minivan
to floss weeds off the engraved name
on a placard—a name getting more
hands, knees at attention
than when s/he were alive
           cornered & confusing
               phantoms for family.

      Now s/he is the phantom,
catered more to in death
than aged irrelevance.

      My mother once lit Newports with lightning
between bong hits of prednisone;

the habit of flavored breath being that hard to break.

Stare at the ground, or mounds of shoveled earth

Now think: What do we really bury?

The soured and sapped chrysalis receipt in her casket,

I was never clear what that was ...
But at least it left enough for us to plant in ritual.

The weakness in our humanity is not letting anything remain buried
long enough.

Years later, a new job w/ a former coworker:

Her first question: *Would I treat her to lunch*
            having forgotten her wallet,
as I'd forgotten melody to song of my own lineage.

Her second inquiry was for references
a list of all my ex's *without including family*
thereby pushing towards me a stack of chips.

I have always been resistant to the obvious.

These are not casino chips, they are bullets
                and this is a trigger warning.

She tells me she was loved once
            but that wasn't the word she used.

A baby cashed out of her womb,
a slot machine clanging human cells.

But what explains me?
Who are my references in bed   in life?
She called for documentation
       on the impact crater weeping stones in my chest

       then watches me load an inherited pistol
       with her words
       aim it at my own head and pull the trigger.

I told her just like I told the dead:
I'd rather be _____
than rent space in any more arms of ashes.

Everything I've loved has led to unmarked holes and wild grasses.

Rain falling over a funeral, the only touch I can stand.

Holes and wild grasses, I said.
       Holes and wild grasses.

74

EIGHTY-EIGHT

There are 88 miles between us
                  rocked raw and dead-ended
                              88 miles of asphalt poured gumbo hot

        meteorite roadkill ignites
        into white phosphorus solar flares
        blurring what's left of Route 66

88 hospice beds   grow wild in a Fibonacci bouquet
                  along Burma Shave highways

88 gray wolves hopscotch the distance
        while the dawn's sun branches
                the horizon like a plum

A squadron of 88 blood moons hover the interstate
                        above a keyboard of crows
                                    pitching eggs like grenades

88 days have passed without incident
        involving unwanted riverbank babies
                begging for bottles in the blackberry bushes

no matter how many flowerbeds I crawl into
they're not as warm as the grave of your final embrace

88 bayous boil down to banks of saltpeter
bringing whole brother-less armies
to their knees in service to shame

88 deltas bubbling crawfish the color of devotion roses—
born again crustaceans pinching hallelujahs from the air

I am one of 88 men staring at a photograph of someone dying
or dead

The body in the photo appears to be melting

its mouth loose as a child's shoestring, yolks leaking from their eyes

I have been here before   standing bedside   awaiting the drop

Unsure what to pray for, I keep clearing my throat

We are not touching—my hands don't know you
so they hang from my arms like sleeping bats

while Death dings off the elevator
holding 88 sunflowers dripping crinkled leaves

I am squinting to focus a memory that has blurred with strangers
            perhaps I should hurry my apology, but where was I
            going with it?

This makes 88 times I thought all scotch was consecrated
while 88 tongues await the unleavened forgiveness of the body

            I smoked 88 blunts
                        at the double-locked door of a no-vacancy church
                                    where god keeps their eyes bashfully shut

I spent 88 Septembers in solitary casinos
            pulling slot machines until one paid out
                        an infant coughing up its own skeleton

                                    88 days have passed
                        and I stay climbing the mountainside
wishing I were a sun you found worthy enough to see rise

THE MASK

(for TRS)

the first mask i ever made was a lie for my mother.
i coughed and sneezed with loneliness; of being a worthless friend to other
boys my age.
she turned and offered to take me somewhere she just remembered,   filled
with children.
this scared me good. being taken to a place and dropped off.
i could be disappeared. telling the truth was expensive.

i went instead to the backyard and constructed my first mask of mud and
motor oil,
grass and dog hair. i needed a new face; one not so lonely.
how proud she would be seeing my loneliness having now passed like a fever.

my next mask was to cover a panic attack for visiting family.
weeks after learning i was adopted i became a stranger to myself, miscast in my
memories.
i sat in my room feeling an imposter. my life belonged to someone else.

eventually, i forged a mask to present at dinner, in church, in class.
a newly risen son ok with the world, its secrets and lies. small price paid for a
furnished life.

my next mask was the only thing handed down from my birth-mother.
i sat in a car next to a woman wanting to gently erase and re-define me.
she handed me a mask i never looked at then drove across town to my new
grandmother's house.

both my grandmothers were dead; yet here stands a third swooning into me.
i let her kiss what she could identify.
i don't know if the mask smiled or was grateful. given no direction
i stood stock still center stage, shallow breathing if i breathed at all
and was pelted with platitudes addressed to a stranger.

i return home to review this alternative life.
my mother asks if i want to demote her; call her something different.
i say no; grateful for a mask that was waterproof.

i can't keep track of all my masks or list what they've hidden;
the dents and damages taken.

sometimes a mask protects you—but mostly it's for others.

one mask lasted 7 funerals. 3 houses. 2 apartments. 1 fire. it has never been
kissed.

there are those who throw off their masks; burn them like bras or draft cards.

i once saw a video of a tree burning from within, smoking like a furnace and
too hot to touch.

i, too, looked normal in the eyes of anyone who claimed to love me but didn't
know my name.
i was asymptomatic to smoke and flame.

on my final day of work in san francisco, i slammed glass after glass of merlot
while watching a cruise ship slowly drift into the turquoise bay. cloudless sky.
the ship a poisoned cake lit with electric candles.

alone at the conference room window, i drank water glasses weeping red wine; a black boy in a white law firm, hiding behind the shine of a paycheck. the ship emerged thru rolling fogbanks of death coughed equally hard by the homeless as by men too entitled to wash their hands in the bathroom and who, by anointing their fingertips first, think their piss blessed and antibacterial.

i stand six feet behind them now, unemployed. for them, i wear a new mask. this one in honor of my grandfather's father's—picnicked from a tree in oklahoma and for whom no mask was ever made or allowed or approved. only one mask was ever made a white man could respect.

many an entitled life has never needed to mask themselves, belonging everywhere. only behind double-locked doors do i dare remove my mask to stare down mirrors, shout into the cave, echoing above my shoulders.

i've worn the mask and am still here. i've worn the mask for family i didn't recognize
to cover the man i failed to become.

i still wear the mask

to remain hidden. to keep peace. to make love. to make money. to barricade screams. to stave off vomit.

IV.

ENTERING THE ATMOSPHERE OF MARTIAN

Do you know the word for this feeling
      where you feel like
a floating satellite,
                or an astronaut
on a spaceship with a dead motor?

You're lonely. A little horny.
      Hallucinating on boredom.

You're millions of miles away from
the scattered billiards of other planets,
all more cold and sterile
      than you've ever felt.

You're millions of miles away from earth, too,
      small enough now for your pocket—

floating miraculously.

And in one blinking moment
as you watch the earth spin

you say to yourself:

I bet not one single person is thinking of
or missing me   right now.

Maybe they did a few minutes ago.

Perhaps they will again, soon.

But in this moment as you stare
helplessly far away—you feel yourself
the sole resident of a sleepy black hole.

So, what is the word for that?

If your tongue knows the texture
and flavor of this feeling,
then what follows is for you.

MARTIAN

After terraforming your night skin into a constellation of succulents
—what else is worth exploring / Tongue sensors / scan new geophysic

language / ultraviolet fingers / in orbit spinning / rockets propelling
sticky dream nipples / through a necklace of star clusters

your black gibbous moons indecisive waxing / waning to and fro /
sleep chanting canticles of milk behind a firewall of denim.

Chocolate meteorites of magnetite and silica / Their solar nutmeg
fusion / their viscous humidity / their orbital launch & vapor

trail spreading nets of munitions / across radiant fields
of sweet hair & bedspreads / like any man at war.

Your pulsar fountain's sparkling applause in comets / every
asteroid impact crater / blasting open / a seed-head of color.

I succumb to zero gravity / my pressure modules splintering
hurtling from heaven / I am touch illiterate / I search for words

in my own mouth / my sweet & sour lunar crater / despite
its post-apocalyptic emptiness / What word best describes an

appetite for exploration of the unknown / Don't say desire / Longing
is a pornographic sir-name in certain galaxies. So / How to read

a map of black holes / How to guess the temperature of your
nearest astronaut / Have you touched an alien life form today?

You got me bout to come / is how I begin all my missions / You got me
curious about what's out there & what flavor it assumes / I could live

on your Tang extract for 8 days / & name each molecule uniquely
after jazz singers / insect species / Jupiter's moons / My mouth could

revive you / tongue your keyboard of nerves / A soft valley of new
life-forms / to restring your upright spinal bass / Psychedelic flowers

to cultivate / weeping yeast for bread to bake / Your eyelashes
& lips bruise me / from inside out / Find me sticky & fibrous.

A moldy peach / shattered by the kitchen floor / I am stone
I am mop / I am swarm of sugared water / a bee shopping

the spires of the giant blue hyssop / lactating sucrose.
            Do you know the origin for the word *testimony*?

Back then, words were valued just that much / What makes
it really strange is how easy its legend is to believe / A row of

soldiers / willing to exchange their balls / if their words fall impotent.
Please note / History's second choice in oathing after *balls* is *bible*.

Perhaps / Adam's balls were filled with the Word of God / or honey
or space dust / I only know / Adam's first prayer was: *It's not you, it's me.*

Was God surprised by Adam as appetizer / his saintly rivulets
of butter / his crunchy Mass of breath / dust & carnal itch?

He named each animal / but there's never been a proper name for
free-range loneliness migrating head to toe / And what did Adam

eat / After naming each animal / did he lick it / check its seasoning?
Who will feed us / if we can't name what we want on a plate?

Fuck You / my first robo-waiter yelled / *I'll need tabs of Viagra and an
extension cord* / I stage-whispered / Me, a quasar / light years from rapture

sitting in a spaceship / as if waiting to be accepted by an alien
official / I had no Voyager discs to DJ / or heart beats to sample.

Just this astronomer's pubic canopy / its rainforest of fresh & fruity
antibiotics / Use me to keep warm / like how you once used a campfire.

You'll need dry / fine tinder / & friction spinning / & grinding / to work
the flame up the ladder / until embers awaken their bright red eyes

& weep smoke / There's been weeping / but no one has touched
me & triggered fire / No touch at all / except to shove my shoulder

as they shower past / blind. If I remain in people's way / I shall be touched
again / Even if touch rhymes with choke / or punch / or shove / it's still touch.

I see sex as a kind of conversation with various sticking points.
My past lovers have been mutes / with mouths full of mirrors

or judges who gavel on / over guilt & sentences / How might you describe
your first love / Clumsy or clever / Stupid or selfish / Or *sad sad sad*?

The sun was first described as / an erupting volcano falling from the sky.
Magmatic / hot to see / *inflamed / brilliant* / cast gold luminous

& swelling upon its approach / darkness parting / in star-crested waves.
The sun itself described the flavor of darkness / how one might explain

skin first tasted / skin not your own / foreign & savory / its seasoned
cells sweating oyster water / Swallowed flames reheat the body's

forgotten science / & wasted fertility / Now, close the cargo doors of the
shuttle / my engine begins firing in deorbit burn / Such complex algebra

just to land in welcoming arms / I emerge from your shadow / dumb as an eclipse
but at least relieved / The world has remained the same / it is me

made glossy with newness / & unanswerable questions / My life:
Untouched / Unloved / Undercover? NO—

Alive & Throbbing & Alone

WHAT REMAINS ETERNAL

a friend
>   a fence

a dog playing catch with rocks

Our names in porch sirens
nightly hymnals pleading into god's velveteen cloak

a clothesline   a rotary phone
a sideboard flaking blue chip stamps

antique flu quilts shedding panels of wintry leaves

a plum switch,
>   a punch bowl
>   a fish tank spray-cleaned on the lawn with a hose

Our valiant pets   medicating prescriptions of grass

and grandpa scratching his sweaty back on a post

Sears catalog
mint and menthol
the spicy mouth of a hushed church purse

                closets gray scaled with uniforms,   shoe shine kits
          rooms grinning in photographs & ceramic chicken dust-catchers

iron skillets,
      sage   bell pepper
     laundry baskets of collards and loud onions

eggs denote spirit—drunken phantasms
drizzling their ectoplasmic art
             down our nicotine-yellow walls

VANISHING TWIN SYNDROME

I.

Birthday cake in blue concentration; cascading broaches of hibiscus sugar-flowers; 9 floating candle-flames shiny as dimes.

II.

A tablescape of children, faces erased digitally or obscured as through nylon, making viewers recall a robbery.

    A. dense, funky collards / mud dauber popsicles / counsel of sticky maple branches / pigeon-toed panthers / elbows ashy + anonymous / inflamed collision of afros sheened / lips purpled from drank /   after drank / bikes triple parked on the porch

III.

SEPTEMBER, 1977

IV.

God's-Eye View of a cantaloupe-patterned kitchen floor. A mother.

A drooling, busy sink. A link of children run diagonally from the dining room towards the backdoor.

V.

Backyard; Children mount a green pick-up truck and it dissolves into a pirate ship under the stage direction of a dirty, barking dog.

VI.

Close-up on one child. This is the Birthday Boy. His skin shiny, new shirt smeared with cake. He triumphantly climbs a bumper.

VII.

From the bumper, Birthday Boy now sees his friend, standing at the chicken wire fence where the driveway ends, holding a gift box.

Further behind his friend, a car idles. A woman smokes.

VIII.

The Birthday Boy leaps from the car and bounds down the driveway, the dog shadowing him quick.

IX.

Two friends stand separated by a simple, homemade fence and a gift box. Birthday Boy is handed the gift box. He opens it.

[SIGNAL LOST - CUT TO BLACK]

VOICE OVER:

i don't have the weather for this—
to rein in all the selves i've been too naive to value
my sky quilting caterpillar shut
    my heart's atonal clumsiness

it's not fear of amputation keeps me from reaching out—
    everything i have is severed;

    it is same fear frost has of the morning sun.
    i, too, sweat mass under dominion
        of certain glances

    i will be abandoned
        where it is dark and untalked about

i am the single twin born twice
a dollop of silver splashed onto a mirror

    standing at this chicken wire threshold
    i stay loyal to a forgotten fraternity

even as this house crumbles into tombstones

and everything: its alphas, omegas
   and their outmoded almanacs
   oxidize into ashes

i am the single twin born twice
     an unfinished whole
 to whom shall i pledge this rosary of orphan tongue-blood?

1.

if you don't mind my terrific thirst
let me lick the pop rocks smudging your palm
this anointment, its makeshift rite of passage
a vaccine for memory sickness
stain of ash after the covenant of brothers

boyhood being a religious science
with expressive ceremonies of high antiquity

hazing backroom marks, chakra spinners
in trues and vogues, big-six bone yards
of body rocking dj squads,
bottles, blunts and backseat hail marys,
sequencers dripping uncleared dna samples,
sideshow smokeouts, BBQ's of vinyl & burned rubber,
sandglass bulbs counting decades in falling dice

if i stick out my tongue
you'd think i'd been lapping blood over sugar

2.

memory moths blink their frantic bellies
noisily against the skull
my heart howls its back-porch blues each midnight
serenading a floating platform of lunar bone
       plated purple and pristine in its brilliant esoterica

beneath the shuffle of Jupiter's tarot moons
an astrological confidence game—
i'm snookered by a hustling zodiac
having never seen the hooded queen

billiards of amalthia and europa
spark eclipses of blood cells
       when colliding over my seventh house

what private never goes soldier
lets the war at home draft him all 10,000 days?
could a rite of passage without bullets
or barrooms lead to a manhood worth saving?
is this plastic ghost possible?
this hollow avatar stalking my reflection

3.

What manner of boy is this?
Bread basket baby, left amongst the milk bottles on our porch

tagged with a name   scribbled quick   in pencil.

      A boy can be broken
and non-returnable, if found depressed, cracked.

We won't get our deposit back.

Lookit this here. Latchkey ingrate. His crib
mattress of unaddressed fan mail to imagined siblings.

He's a balloon hammer. Throw a ball, he'll duck.

Bad dog. Bad boy. Worthless reservist.

Voodoo priest trading cards slap his bike spokes.

Greed s'posed to look good on boys his age;
                tongue-tied whenever truth's at stake.

Bench-warming bitch.   He's a tool

with nowhere to hang

in my shed.

4.

forget shadow contracts in mud, spit, blade
forget clamshell promises slapped tight
dynamite honeycomb hideouts

in cherry bomb blunt smoke

children get divorced, too and told

Sign here. Stop it.
Show me your hand.
Show me your heart.
Show me where it hurts.

pick a switch from the tree with the blackest
shade and come here

5.

remaining loyal to bad habits
i hold this lotus at your throat
like a knife   robbing your pockets
of sandalwood & suede, snatch

your flashy cinnamon aura
            to backtrack the formula
that made you

this a prayer in reverse
                  where i genuflect & fill myself
with your aromatic grapefruit lather
your magnolia white pepper musk

in butterfly language
there's no word for grief

so their floating devotionals
trigger me to feed them from my eyes

memory happens like this

a pond of contemplative pigeons
on the sidewalk

shattering the air around you at once

wings whipping in their panicked festival

what dusty pictures arise?

you never had control
you always had choice

6. {Invention of Intimacy}

We liked one another better than our fathers liked us.
Our favorite stories were always myths involving the vanquished: soldiers
eaten down to the bone, cities exploding at the feet of waltzing monsters,
wrestlers shoving, kneading, adjusting another's will—mechanics of pain.

We jump-started together once we realized blood had flavor,
anything with aroma:

A plastic action figure   A ribbon of ripped fabric   A golden thigh

A spray of hair, its bushy rabbit.

The soft medicinal roux of a tongue tracing, folding
    —Greco-Roman pantomimes—
Touch me like you're blind. My ribs, my spine rhyme in braille.
Punctuation in hair, tiny commas stuttering periods on sentences
left incomplete.
Thought bubbles hiccup ellipses, flashing fingers trigger a seizure in giggles.

On the tarot card, The Tower, 'twas a joke sent everything tumbling.

Is this too inside, like short-clothes seasoned for laundry?

Red briefs, rare interior
scalding broth spilling
spraying, springs droplets.

Boys armed with flowers
promoted to guns or swords
beaten senseless on the fence post.

Dancing dirty auditioning for hell—
nasty as shovels for ditches
or spoons still needing to be licked.

7.

excuse my touch and its primal directive

these fleshy antennae scan melodic frequencies midair

      beatbox djembes
            the yelp of rubber soles
breaking Mach 1 on the court
                in the dark
                in the seams
                underground

beneath the tulips, their ticklish roots
trace back to a technicolor heart—
a convict beating against his bone cage

      nothing wild waits
      or stands on ceremony

since winning is at stake
i won't be picked this round

a certain scream haunts my silences

lightning struck once
now i chase every cloud
throwing keys in delicious stupidity

this fraternal rite was a hoax from jump
a spam love letter from a Russian bot
        no fire burns here
        the element needed
        to fuse us together
        hasn't been discovered

no fire burns here
yet i am consumed
down to the red sketch
of my skeleton

beneath this squall of sweat
i disco ball

i don't want to say anything
i want something said to me

it's why i once ran to a psychic
who described my spirit
as disrobing my body
an adolescent slouching
out of overalls

it made him laugh mid-reading
this unveiling
an aura in clown drag
even as it explained perpetual motion

a heart falling through time

8.

boys eat gravel
spit lit matches in fireworks
or fortune telling

first tattoos of flame hushed by bandages of butter
first piercings of rebar and canines
first brandings with Monkey Ward's leather

jawbreakers paid with a currency of scabs
peeled skin banana'd back into place

sealed with tribal scars and slashes to ward off death
despite cherry sweet blood defrosted, leaking

pornographic vapor of rough-housing mutts
        sensing the moon about to crest;   fanged, thirsty
        inventing capoeira in cardboard arenas of bone dust

9.

born clean from my mother,
daily i dress myself in mud & axel grease
fishskin & coyote blood

birds see me as the herald of death
kicking the confinements of silence

i dent every frame
crack every shell   test every system

even this cluster of nerves,
... the last on earth.

if nothing gets tested
how will you know anything works?

i perfectly dismantle anything unbroken
break land speed records on my Schwinn.
bionic with skill   i can fly

this body awarded with stitches.

every weekend i am thrown together again
in my father's Golgotha

says he brought me here
and wants his money's worth

and his word is BOND
                                        not SORRY.

he thumps sorry words out my mouth,
words i suck too hard, like bad candy.

he always say: *love makes men weak.*
save that word for when you start your first fire
nobody can put out.

10. {Heirloom Noodles}

He and I share mothers,
but entirely different creation stories.

Three Fridays after she died
we meet for dinner at a mirror-walled restaurant;

its dervish of steaming platters,
noodles taffy-pulled at the door.

This feels like an affair I want to kick away from

but he's the only one who remembers me
      as if my life really did happen.

I don't like who I am with him.
We both should be different.

We—neither of us—will speak in honest diagnoses
of soured rooms,   the body's dark indifferent magic

how breath, sometimes, will leave a path of bruises

or how people frost & drop off the vine while you watch,
your hands pocketed, clean.

Having buried one mother already,
I know this territory—

my hands salted from 100 nights of fever.

      A brother should tell another what's coming
as much as what's been.

I've rehearsed this meal for days now
but after sitting with him, I forgot my line.

We play catch with silence & trivia.

A crash of salt pelts the edge of his plate,
rimshot to the corniest of jokes.

Awkward intimacy between men—
                how we punch the confines of our closest embraces.

11. {Shotgun Scrub}

cock diesel mustang
its gravelly oration in afterburn
its threat display pawing up asphalt
greeting night rain with kerosene

why isn't this orangesicle sunrise
melting over our private interstate
preferable to a stroke of arcade cabinets
choking on tokens

fuck it—pour two more fingers of leaded petrol
and keep an eye on that dead clock—
you know I got silences back home to feed

no chick should peep alone
                yet anyone with me is alone, amirite?
but you ain't trying to hear that, G.

despite our dapping hands
slamming shots
shuffling points
despite daybreak coming on like a headache

twin gold marlboros: one lit, one hushed
sun & moon
streetlights jump from puddle to hood polish

contrails and castles of conjured smoke
growl, snort
black & mild
intersection red-assed
tagged wild style
melody of E&J bottles in avalanche of applause

—a sigh stalls in my throat
admiring the wound the sky has made
while kites dip stupidly along the marina

PROOF

My body has a legend, he says
midstory, and wipes his mouth.

Then, as to recite grace,
stands at the table to prove it.

Beneath the drape of his shirt
a savana of skin ripples slightly.

For a blink, i don't understand
what's missing:

He had no belly button,
            his stomach paved mythologically clean.

We'd been so casual
playing catch with origin stories
                                after class
            over crepes and pancakes,
our roll call of scars.

We'd been speaking of doctors and mistakes
when his face shifted gears,

he landed his fork like tapping a baton.

This is how boys are. Show
and prove.   Tale of the tape.

People are terrified by skin
          not meeting their expectations.

For years, white women were forbidden
from showing their navels on TV.
The networks were alarmed
                    over what they symbolized,
                         how they seemed to prove something,
          root us together.

Seeing the placenta as nebula
          a star-field of skin
                    a chandelier from which
                    we're all suspended
flaring out from the same light.

If men can write shame laws over belly buttons

it's no surprise the fumbling
of a Black child
steaming new and helpless
in a cage of fingers.

A rabbit *midwifed* by a hawk.

                    I know this now.

Yet, how I doubted him, Lord.

My sticky, maple fingers trembled in prayer all night.

A TASTE
OF AMNIOTIC FLUID

milky floral buds

        snap open
        traps broken

pistil pores pop

            push out

a porridge of sautéed cells
            melted to malted—

globules of grease
                molded to the body

        sends me further
        down the street

                    than I'd ever gone before

dizzy   with questions
unspeakable, unanswerable

my brains compass

                    a helicopter
                            of dandelion
petals   spinning
            over estates of skin

boiling in upheaval
            itch of cascading petals

primer of tongues   tickling touch

tearing like a lucid dream animal

                    through the black chaparral

BOYS AND STRANGER

fat and lonely

    skinny and light

        zipper and laughing

famished and you

    story and new (memories)

        wheatgrass and flu

vaccine and further

    himself and leaves

        Jagermeister and Newports

park and stop

    Mission and nervously

        roommate and ask

door and doesn't

in and shut

        talking and pacing

you and you

        here and wish

                shirt and cheek

nose and face

        up and turn

                noisy and alive

twinkling and watery

        frown and wipe

                warm, and full

A VIRGIN SPEAKS ON ACCIDENTAL INTIMACY

                                        Her white house

its weekend gallery of gamers   stoned
snorers scattered across twin couches.

I share the last Murphy bed
fenced in by a minaret of beer bottles

next to my Best Friend.

          The bed shifts,
sheets sigh an ocean's spray.

The shoe he had been   wearing (?)
                                         holding (?)

somehow   slams against the wall   I was facing.

Then, his sequoia-throwing arm settles over me.

I play possum-dead.

Slept, he did, like a barnacle

                            dense,   briny

before   running knuckles   up my back.

I lay waiting   for breath

                        to moves

when I feel him whitecap the air

                               rise, turn

        deep-dive the bed's farthest port

(an aurora borealis of the mind)

sleep-mumbling:

                 Wrong person.

The whole frame squeaks in agreement.

He levels deeper,

                dissolving easily as sugar.

        I watch him

               go.

HUG

Both visiting days he asked for this
           his prophetic eyes, body
                    a Catherine wheel going nova:

first, vaulting off the parallel bars of his walker

next, holy ghost dismounting the bed

a 10-point landing on the terrace
                         of my chest.

In the agreed-upon silence of my arms

           he felt fractional.
His spine floated, overcooked
                       beneath his skin.

We whispered
        as if healing
were a current
        directed by harmonized wavelets
of breath.

Anyone watching might've expected
                 us to kiss
since we appeared to eclipse something.

Pulling open the door,
                    I turned.

How quiet and humble he looked.

Hollow,
            drowsy as a toddler.

The room   glittered,

a stainless steel fish tank.

                He, a betta   crown-tailed by illness.

Seeing him   centered

                        floating

                gulping air

                    like that.

CONDEMNED

Let me revel in the ruins of your body.
It's not enough being a hack comedian
at the dry rotting masonry of your feet
while foreign hymns timidly drift-in from intensive care.

I'd rather be your spectral inspector
sipping a mug of ectoplasmic mocha
while excavators chew the bitter licorice
of your far off rooms—

      banshees screaming thought balloons of diesel

hydraulic giraffes   crash of rhinos   chewing your joists
down to boneblack—lipping plaster like cake frosting
off exposed veneers branching at wild angles.

Surfing your quaking kitchen, I scream:
Is anyone going to lunch? I have a punch-list
of possible sandwiches!   then pretend
its my voice pounding apertures
through your plaster walls.

I collect rattling appliances in a black wheelbarrow
while chandeliers spit emergency sirens of light.

To think your cathedral was once a tree

its stained-glass, a beach
and these modest portholes the only way
by which you share or receive any love.

These elegantly arched stairwells helix to your failing heart.

Let me be winning bid and final contractor.
Let me be your gray-powder ghost of sheetrock.
Let me be the last gust of wind, slamming you closed.

DURING THE PARADE

It was startling to see you
staring out from a touchpad
on the ground.

Your mouth's silent cloud.
You blinked bewildered
a patient newscaster.

You appeared engaged
even as people stepped over
you, and confetti misted.

I wept, picking up the screen.
How'd you get here, I asked.
My mom dropped me off, you said.

You smiled. You wore a 1950s
fedora. You looked nice.
I scanned the crowd for your mother

but it blurred with strangers. I wondered
if she was somewhere drunk and relieved.
I held you like an empty plate.

I couldn't look in your face.
I wanted to position you
up high somewhere

so you could see everything.
But you only asked me
to hold you.

I WAS A HERO ONCE

A dormant satellite in a room
with children, bouncing
atoms off the walls.
They are faceless, sweaty
and every storm-based verb.
I corral them before the television—
an antique microwave cooking
colorless cartoons.
As the constellation of them settle,
I move to the next room and see it.

The ceramic planter which held
a tittering ficus
had been kicked into slices.
This sight weakens me
into obscene prayers while
pulling shards from the black
pudding soil as if harvesting tombstones.
I caress the threads of roots,
squiggling in my fingers,
like the hand of a dying grandparent—
my heart pours itself empty
through disbelieving eyes.

And to think I was a hero once.

I followed a pack of thieves
who hid in a darkness unnamed by science,
yet I could still see them
            and felt sorry for them
as I levitated above the yard.
The stitching in my palms itched
emitting ophidian beams of flame
igniting every wet, incombustible
thing, synthesizing everything else
to greasy ash.

                I could not be defeated.
I was so alone.

            And look at me now:

Stacking broken pottery,
pawing through soil as hissing
tears drop like dead moths.

Only a _____ can be bested
and crushed from within by indifferent children.

reading guide

Theme: **AMERICA**

1. **U HAVE THE RIGHT** is based on the
Miranda rights.

- o What are *the Miranda rights*? How are they used?
- o Who is the You being addressed? Who is speaking?
- o Is this an angry poem? Why or why not?

2. **FOUND POEM: BAD APPLES** is written after an
article from *off-guardian* by Edward Curtain, "The Satanic
Nature of The Bombings of Hiroshima and Nagasaki." From
August 6 to August 9, 1945, between two hundred and three
hundred thousand Japanese civilians were intentionally killed
with atomic bombs made and delivered from America.

- o Why? Describe an appropriate alternative to bombing.
- o What is the value of a bomb?
- o When does a bomb come in handy?
- o How would the world be if bombs were never invented?

3. Read the poem **AMERICA, I AM**:

- Fill in the blank: I am proud to be a/an _____ .
- When is it appropriate to call oneself an American?
- From the poem, what is being referenced in the line: "As for ya'll tired, / ya'll poor / ya'll huddled masses/ yearning to breathe free"?

4. What is being referred to in the poem **IF YOU SEE SOMETHING, SAY SOMETHING**?

- What is the difference between slavery and oppression?
- Is it better or easier to oppress adults or children?
- Under what circumstances are children oppressed?

5. Read the poem **BULLET GUMBO**:

- What is a "gumbo"?
- What is a "gun show"?
- Describe your experience with guns.
- What are you being taught about guns in America?
- In the poem, what does the "Grandmomma" represent?
- Do guns kill people?

6. Read Allen Ginsberg's original poem, "America" (1956).

   o What is the difference between that and the poem,
**BETWEEN A ROCK WALL AND
AN IMMIGRANT**?

7. The first line of **BETWEEN A ROCK WALL AND
AN IMMIGRANT** refers to a song by Nina Simone,
"Mississippi Goddam."

   o Listen to the song and describe what it is about? Can you
write a poetic answer to that song?

   o Describe "freedom" as it is found in America.

Theme: THE PERSONAL AND THE QUOTIDIAN

1. Write a celebratory poem about something mundane you do every day:

- Write a poem about standing in line.
- Write a poem for a person you see regularly but don't know personally (a bus driver, a barista, a commuter).
- What is the smallest item you can write a poem about? Consider a fingernail, a coin, a leaf.

See the poems: **SATURNALIA**

INTERVIEW WITH A ROSE

ODE TO A DESICCATED OLIVE

HUG

ODE TO MY TOWEL

2. Write a poem about being self-conscious or embarrassed.

See the poems: **PERSONAL FOREST, THE MASK**

3. Write a poem about a "secret place."

- Consider a "secret place" that's not yours? Why is it secret?

See the poems: **TOGUNA AT 61ST AND MARKET**

HOUSE OF SLAMS AND HOLLERS

FINANCIAL DISTRICT CONFESSIONS

4. Consider someone close to you: a parent, partner, or relative. Write a poem describing them at work or doing something they are passionate about.

See the poem: **HOW TO OPERATE HEAVY MACHINERY (CIRCA 1978)**

5. What should never be spoken aloud?

o Imagine a poem or story where someone confesses or owns up to something.

See the poems: **FINANCIAL DISTRICT CONFESSIONS**

PERSONAL FOREST

SHOTGUN SCRUB

6. Write a poem about the awkward distances between people.

o Write a poem or story about two people or entities who are NOT listening to one another.

o What does it mean to *speak truth*, yet not be heard?

See the poems: **EIGHTY-EIGHT**

**VANISHING TWIN SYNDROME: 10.
{HEIRLOOM NOODLES}**

TRIGGER WARNING

7. Write a poem about a specific place (house, room, church, yard, etc.) but only mention the items found within it.

See the poems: **WHAT REMAINS ETERNAL**

A TASTE OF AMNIOTIC FLUID

BOYS AND STRANGER

8. Everything ends. Nothing is eternal.

o   Write a poem for something you wish would last forever.

See the poems: **VANISHING TWIN SYNDROME**

HUG

CONDEMNED

ODE TO A DESICCATED OLIVE

Theme: **ART OF & IN LIFE**

1. Search for the original digital print, **HER MAJESTY QUEEN SOFIE**, by artist Mary Sibane.

- Who is Queen Sofie?
- Is this an appropriate opening poem for *Martian: The Saint of Loneliness*? Why or why not?

2. The title of the poem **PHANTOM PAIN** uses the phrase associated with the sensation of having something such as a "phantom limb."

- What is a "phantom limb"?
- Who is the "I" in the poem? Why might the "I" call itself an artist?
- Discuss the following line from the poem: "In most families, men are as easy to lose as keys or lighters."
- Visit a local museum or gallery and choose a work of art that attracts you. Write a response or story to it.
- Try writing a poem dedicated to something specific or unusual, i.e, a sculpture, installation, texture, sound, color, or title of a work.

See the poems: **PHANTOM PAIN**

QUESTIONS FOR ART STUDY

notes & acknowledgments

HER MAJESTY QUEEN SOPHIE was published in *Barzak*, 2019. It was written after work of the same name by Mary Sibane, for San Francisco's Museum of the African Diaspora (MOAD), 2018.

U HAVE THE RIGHT was published in 2019 in *Civil Liberties United*, edited by Shizue Siegel. Written after the *Miranda rights*, a phantom line opens the poem: **MY NAME IS JAMES CAGNEY. I AM A POET AND I REFUSE TO REMAIN SILENT WHILE THIS NATION CONTINUES TO MURDER BLACK PEOPLE. I HAVE A RIGHT TO BE ANGRY.** This was a trending Facebook event invented by members of the African American poets organization, Cave Canem. Colleagues were writing and reading protest poems then posting videos online. I drafted the poem during trips for acupuncture treatment on my arthritic knee. The office was a four-block walk from the BART station, and my knee made those blocks painfully long. So, I'd focus on poetry instead of pain and dictated lines into my phone. I wrote more lines than I needed, then cut them down into a form I thought worked.

FOUND IN AMERICA: BAD APPLES is a found poem. Its text originates from an 2018 article by Edward Curtain, "The Satanic

Nature of The Atomic Bombings of Hiroshima and Nagasaki."
https://off-guardian.org/2018/08/07/the-satanic-nature-of-
the-atomic-bombings-of-hiroshima-and-nagasaki. While reading
I copied some of Curtain's sentences into a word file, then later
returned to those sentences and played with them, by reorganizing,
cutting, and commenting. Consider this a personal edit and
rewrite of his article.

AMERICA, I AM was published in a limited edition chapbook,
Colossus: Bay Area Poets Challenge Immigration Injustice, edited by
Sara Biel and Karla Brundage, 2018. The title amuses me as it implies
a pattern or form that the poem itself never follows.

IF YOU SEE SOMETHING, SAY SOMETHING was
published in *The Maynard*, 2018. Written in the Patrice Lumumba
Poets Workshop at Eastside Arts Alliance, its structure is my own
invention. Write a stanza of 4–5 lines, then blow up and reconstruct
that stanza four more times, pushing and varying word use as needed.

In 2012, my friend artist Natasha Marin curated a group of a dozen
artists to share our work at galleries in Mumbai, India. A small part
of my performance was to interview random guests at our event.
During one interview, I asked someone: "Is there anything you'd like
to ask America?" He said, "Yes. Is it true in America, guns don't kill
people? Because when I think of America, I think gun." What would
your answer have been? It took a couple of years to write my answer,
BULLET GUMBO. I never wanted to write such a thing but
felt bullied into it by social media, the news, and the youth marches
against gun violence shutting down traffic in front of the office where
I worked.

BETWEEN A ROCK WALL AND AN IMMIGRANT
was published in *Civil Liberties United* in 2019. It was written in
response to the death of Jakelin Amei Rosmery Caal Maquin, a
seven-year-old girl who died in the custody of US Customs and
Border Protection in 2018. The poem is modelled after Allen
Ginsberg's 1956 poem, "America." The line "There I Go" refers to the
song "There I Go, There I Go Again" by Eddie Jefferson. My poetry
colleagues sampled that line and its melody a lot at open mics in
Oakland in the 1990s.

PHANTOM PAIN and **QUESTIONS FOR ART
STUDY** are ekphrastic poems developed at the Museum of the
African Diaspora (MOAD) in San Francisco in 2017. Special thank
you to Arisa White, Elizabeth Gessel, and the staff at MOAD. Both
poems were written simultaneously and communicate with one
another. They contain trace elements of several paintings displayed in
MOAD's gallery that season.

LOVE IS EASIER THE HEADLESS WAY is another
ekphrastic poem after Rene Magritte's *Le Duo* (The Lovers), 1928.
It was written during a writers workshop at Berkeley Art Museum
curated by poet MK Chavez where we were tasked to choose
a painting and write a poem after it. It was published, along with
ODE TO A DESICCATED OLIVE in *The Maynard*, 2018.
The "Olive" in question was given to me by a very chatty
vendor at the Galleria Farmers Market in San Francisco, where I
bought honey and lemons. I don't enjoy olives but kept the sample he
once gave me, and let it dry out at my desk at work. I still have it.

THE MASK—During the coronavirus quarantine, a friend asked
if I'd write something inspired by Paul Laurence Dunbar's poem,

"We Wear The Mask." I did. He immediately returned my mediocre remix of Dunbar's original, explaining he'd rather have something more personal, something only I could write. Once I started writing this, I nearly couldn't stop.

INTERVIEW WITH A ROSE—During the work day, a poet sits at a quiet reception desk and stares at a rose.

ODE TO MY TOWEL—If Neruda wrote one, I didn't find it. But what I learned from him is the importance of observing with loving attention all our tiny, overlooked things.

PERSONAL FOREST—For a while, I was an itchy child. I remember sitting in class as a 5th grader, and finding a single long hair at my Adam's apple. By seventh grade I had a full beard and often had to pay adult fare on the bus. Magazines and TV made adolescent me self-conscious about being hairy. All the models in magazine spreads and on TV were slick as sports cars. Turns out, no one saw anyone naked in the junior high gym as the showers remained dry and unused during my classes.

TOGUNA AT 61ST AND MARKET—*Toguna* is a word from the Dogon people of Mali, West Africa. It means "a community meeting hut," primarily for male village elders. It is intentionally built with a low roof forcing visitors to humble themselves and sit. Anyone rising too quickly in anger or excitement, will hit his head on the low beams and be swiftly returned to peace. After learning about this, I recalled one of the times I rode with my father to a neighborhood filled with men he'd worked with and known for years. Five or seven men sat in a circle in a living room smoking and drinking and talking until the son of the man's house it was came home from school and led me into the backyard. Inexplicably, this poem was featured in a City of Oakland Cultural Affairs Commission meeting in 2020.

HOUSE OF SLAMS AND HOLLERS—If the legend is to be believed and Robert Johnson sold his soul at the crossroads, what did the neighborhood nearest the crossroads look like? I imagined something like the modest neighborhood where my father's Uncle Iley lived, in Delano, California, in the late 70s early 80s. It was a house I'd only been to twice, no more than three times—and one of those visits Uncle Iley wasn't home and we left. I remember unpaved roads and a row of small houses across from a dry creek bed.

HOW TO OPERATE HEAVY MACHINERY—I often think of my father working alone in the garage as a mechanic and my being too young and afraid to ask what he was doing or start any conversations with him. Sometimes I would stand at the bedroom window which overlooked the entire backyard and watch him. I didn't learn to drive until a few years after he died.

FINANCIAL DISTRICT CONFESSIONS—The first law firm I ever worked for gave me some emotionally difficult years. This poem comes from the strangest year when the office moved from one building to another. I was on the team clearing, labelling, and destroying files in the old place. A couple years later, a friend who worked in the same office, would laugh at me over how little work I seemed to do during the day. Almost daily, my boss would call me into his office to talk over movie trivia since I knew a lot, and at the time he was obsessed with Spaghetti Westerns. John Ford never directed any Italian Westerns per se, but he set the standard for the genre and his name was a perfect fit for the poem.

WICKED GAME—My last visit to Oklahoma with my mother was for a family funeral. I spent much of that weekend with my cousin, whom I adored, but who was having a doubly difficult time. He was in the midst of a breakup with his girlfriend, and I offered little empathy as at that time I'd never had a girlfriend. Our weekend together was friendly but somber. I liked the Chris Isaak song this poem is named after and by the time it came on the radio, we'd been driving in silence for quite some time.

TRIGGER WARNING and **I WAS A HERO ONCE** were both published by *Silver Pinion*, 2019. **TRIGGER WARNING** has trace elements of the aforementioned family funeral I attended with my adoptive mom in Oklahoma.

EIGHTY-EIGHT—Approximate number of miles between San Francisco where I worked and Sacramento where my birth mother was, at that time, dying. The poem was published in *As Of Late IV*, 2021.

The only reason to explain and introduce a poem on mic is to quell the speaker's nerves. My nerves were fried before publicly reading **MARTIAN** for the first time. But after one reading, a friend touched my arm and said how that evening's freestyle introduction could make a poem itself. This is why **ENTERING THE ATMOSPHERE OF MARTIAN** exists. It is an appropriate mood setter for **MARTIAN** and is itself a fair poem, and I would like for you to read it.

A different, yet equally wonderful version of **MARTIAN** was published by *Inscape Journal*, 2018. I cannot explain my need to rewrite a 'fine' and published poem except to say I am a poet and that happens. The version appearing in this book is my preferred final.

WHAT REMAINS ETERNAL—Published in *Colossus: Home*, 2020, edited by Sara Biel and Karla Brundage. *Colossus* is an anthology benefitting Moms4Housing and engaged the housing crisis in Oakland. The anthology was published in support of a collective of Black women who were publically evicted the day after Christmas from an unoccupied house in West Oakland. This poem is a list of images and lost objects from my childhood.

VANISHING TWIN SYNDROME—Before the invention of ultrasound, in a twin pregnancy, if one child miscarries without the mother or doctor's knowledge, the tissue of the "vanished twin" will be reabsorbed by the mother and the remaining baby. For an adoptee and poet, this is a fascinating concept to mull over. I may have been eleven or twelve when I had my last real birthday party and when I last saw Anthony, the first close friend I remember having. For me as an only child, he was a kind of surrogate brother. We were so young, I could never recall his last name and attempt to comb through social media for him or his family. Over the years, every fifteen months or so, my brain would flashback to that final day I saw him. While in quarantine, I recalled many friendships I honored (read: loved) but could never maintain. I decided to turn toward what bothered me and write it out. I attempted a crown of sonnets, but my feelings were messier and bigger than the form would allow, so I yielded to free verse, allowing the poem to swing and land where it wanted. Frederico Lorca's poem "A Trip To The Moon" was incredibly helpful, as was John Murillo's sonnet sequence in his book, *Kontemporary Amerikan Poetry*, 2020.

PROOF was published in *Alta*, 2021. That cafe near the UC Berkeley campus made some of the best pancakes I've eaten—TO THIS DAY.

TASTE OF AMNIOTIC FLUID—Published in Noah Sander's *The Racket Quarantine Journal*, 2020.

BOYS AND STRANGER—An erasure poem in which I wrote much too personal an essay to publicly share but kept all words surrounding the conjunction "and."

A VIRGIN SPEAKS ON ACCIDENTAL INTIMACY—Published in *The Racket Quarantine Journal*, 2020.

CONDEMNED—My friend once told me a story of breaking into a house while it was being demolished. I watched this same person stand at the bedside of our mutual friend on her deathbed, several days before her exit, and attempt stand-up comedy since there was nothing else left to say. While sitting by the door of the hospital room, I could hear from down the hall a group of voices singing a psalm in a foreign language.

DURING THE PARADE and **HUG** were published by Noah Sanders in *The Racket Quarantine Journal*, 2020. Both poems are dedicated to my lifelong friend, Sekou Nitoto. **PARADE** was a dream wherein he appeared (himself being an incredibly vivid dream-storyteller) and **HUG** concerns the last time I visited him in hospital. He suffered from Sickle Cell anemia and died early in the coronavirus pandemic.

Despite **I WAS A HERO ONCE** being the description of a dream, it didn't gel as a poem until I added an element from a second dream I had on a different night.

Yes, **SATURNALIA**, yes.

Thank you to the editors of all the journals cited.

Thank you: Michaela Mullin, J. K. Fowler, and all the staff at
Nomadic Press.

Remembering:

Q. R. Hand
Jack Hirschman
Sekou Nitoto
Richard Sanderell
Al Young

Thank you.

JAMES CAGNEY

James Cagney is a writer from Oakland, California. Primarily a self-taught poet, he is the author of two collections. His first, *Black Steel Magnolias in the Hour of Chaos Theory*, won the 2019 PEN Oakland Josephine Miles Award. Cagney's second book, *Martian: The Saint of Loneliness*, was the winner of the 2021 James Laughlin Award from the Academy of American Poets. He is a Cave Canem Fellow. For more writing, visit TheDirtyRat.blog.

JAMESCAGNEYPOET.COM

@REAL_JAMES_CAGNEY

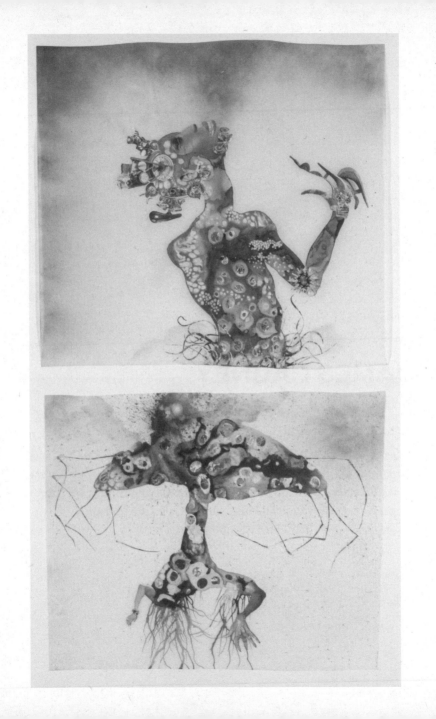

cover art

Living Through Strange Times (2004)
by Wangechi Mutu

Mixed media ink, collage on mylar
38 x 42 in. and 29 x 35 in. (Diptych)
© Wangechi Mutu
Courtesy of the Artist and Gladstone Gallery

Nomadic Press Emergency Fund

Nomadic Press Black Writers Fund

RIGHT BEFORE LABOR DAY 2020 (AND IN RESPONSE TO THE EFFECTS OF COVID), NOMADIC PRESS LAUNCHED ITS EMERGENCY FUND, A FOREVER FUND MEANT TO SUPPORT NOMADIC PRESS-PUBLISHED WRITERS WHO HAVE NO INCOME, ARE UNEMPLOYED, DON'T QUALIFY FOR UNEMPLOYMENT, HAVE NO HEALTHCARE, OR ARE JUST GENERALLY IN NEED OF COVERING UNEXPECTED OR IMPACTFUL EXPENSES.

FUNDS ARE FIRST COME, FIRST SERVE, AND ARE AVAILABLE AS LONG AS THERE IS MONEY IN THE ACCOUNT, AND THERE IS A DIGNITY-CENTERED INTERNAL APPLICATION THAT INTERESTED FOLKS SUBMIT. DISBURSE-MENTS ARE MADE FOR ANY AMOUNT UP TO $300.

ALL DONATIONS MADE TO THIS FUND ARE KEPT IN A SEPARATE ACCOUNT. THE NOMADIC PRESS EMERGENCY FUND (NPEF) ACCOUNT AND ASSOCIATED PROCESSES (LIKE THE APPLICATION) ARE OVERSEEN BY NOMADIC PRESS AUTHORS AND THE GROUP MEETS EVERY MONTH.

ON JUNETEENTH (JUNE 19) 2020, NOMADIC PRESS LAUNCHED THE NOMADIC PRESS BLACK WRITERS FUND (NPBWF), A FOREVER FUND THAT WILL BE DIRECTLY BUILT INTO THE FABRIC OF OUR ORGANIZATION FOR AS LONG AS NOMADIC PRESS EXISTS AND PUTS ADDITIONAL MONIES DIRECTLY INTO THE POCKETS OF OUR BLACK WRITERS AT THE END OF EACH YEAR.

HERE IS HOW IT WORKS:

$1 OF EACH BOOK SALE GOES INTO THE FUND.

AT THE END OF EACH YEAR, ALL NOMADIC PRESS AUTHORS HAVE THE OPPORTUNITY TO VOLUNTARILY DONATE NONE, PART, OR ALL OF THEIR ROYALTIES TO THE FUND.

ANYONE FROM OUR LARGER COMMUNITIES CAN DONATE TO THE FUND. THIS IS WHERE YOU COME IN!

AT THE END OF THE YEAR, WHATEVER MONIES ARE IN THE FUND WILL BE EVENLY DISTRIBUTED TO ALL BLACK NOMADIC PRESS AUTHORS THAT HAVE BEEN PUBLISHED BY THE DATE OF DISBURSEMENT (MID-TO-LATE DECEMBER).

THE FUND (AND ASSOCIATED, SEPARATE BANK ACCOUNT) HAS AN OVERSIGHT TEAM COMPRISED OF FOUR AUTHORS (AYODELE NZINGA, DANIEL B. SUMMERHILL, DAZIE GREGO-SYKES, AND ODELIA YOUNGE) + NOMADIC PRESS EXECUTIVE DIRECTOR J. K. FOWLER.

Please consider supporting these funds. You can also more generally support Nomadic Press by donating to our general fund via nomadicpress.org/donate and by continuing to buy our books.

As always, thank you for your support!

SCAN THE QR CODE FOR MORE INFORMATION AND/OR TO DONATE.

YOU CAN ALSO DONATE AT NOMADICPRESS.ORG/STORE.